# About the Author

David Wilshin has worked as a chef in the UK, Spain and the Caribbean. He has been general manager of the Cambridge Cheese Company since 2002, sourcing and selling fine, artisan foods from around Europe and the world.

He lives in Ely, Cambridgeshire, with his wife, two daughters, Jack Russell terrier and chickens.

# Dedication

For Mum – you always believed in me x

# DAVID WILSHIN

# 52

## A Year of Recipes to Share with Family and Friends

AUSTIN MACAULEY PUBLISHERS™

LONDON • CAMBRIDGE • NEW YORK • SHARJAH

A CIP catalogue record for this title is available from the British Library.

ISBN 978-1-52892-248-7 (Paperback)
ISBN 978-1-52892-250-0 (E-Book)
www.austinmacauley.com

First Published (2019)
Austin Macauley Publishers Ltd
25 Canada Square
Canary Wharf
London
E14 5LQ

# Acknowledgements

Special thanks to everyone at Team Cheese – especially to Paul and Jacky for introducing me to a whole new world of food, and to Jade, Camilla and Shannon for their help with recipes and photos.

# Recipes

# Introduction

We don't stop enough these days. We spend our whole lives rushing around: back and forth to work, school, social gatherings, the gym, yoga, classes, clubs and whatever else we do to fill our time. We spend so much time rushing around that, before we know it, we've become strangers to those around us, each of us just rushing around in our own busy bubble! On the rare occasions we do actually make the effort to sit down, have a nice meal and spend some time together, we inevitably say, 'That was nice – we must do this more often...' – and then promptly forget about it and slip back into the relentless flow of our hectic lives!

Life in the modern world *is* hectic! Sitting down together to dinner every night is, for most of us, an unrealistic aspiration. But if we can find the time just once a week to get together and 'chew the fat', then our lives would be all the better for it!

The aim of this book is to provide you with the inspiration to do just that. It has no particular theme; there are recipes from all over the world, some very simple, some a bit more complicated. You won't find pages of narrative; it's simply a book of ideas. You can dip in and out of it at any time and hopefully find something new and exciting to get your taste buds tingling. But if you do choose to follow it in order, then the 52 recipes will guide you through the culinary calendar, making use of whatever seasonal ingredients are at their best.

Some of the ingredients I've used are unapologetically obscure – I've tried to include alternatives where applicable, but feel free to replace them with something else. Above all, don't be scared to experiment and adapt – that's half the fun!

All recipes serve four unless stated otherwise, but again, feel free to adjust the amounts, depending on how many you're feeding or who you're feeding.

I sincerely hope my enthusiasm shines through in the recipes and that you, and your family and friends, enjoy it as much as I have!

# 1 Fen Celery and Stilton Soup

Protected from the winter frosts by dark peaty soil, lovingly piled around it as it grows, fen celery develops a unique, nutty-sweet flavour and its characteristic crunchy, pale sticks. It is the perfect partner for any left-over Christmas Stilton, for a warming supper that's not too heavy after all the festivities.

**50g butter**

**1 head of fen celery, rinsed well and thinly chopped (reserve some leaves as a garnish)**

**1 small onion, finely chopped**

**1 leek, thinly sliced**

**200g potatoes, peeled and diced into small cubes**

**750ml chicken stock**

**150ml double cream**

**200g Stilton cheese, crumbled in your fingers**

**Ground black pepper and plenty of granary bread rolls and butter to serve**

1. Melt the butter in a decent sized saucepan on a medium heat. Add the celery, onion, leek and potato and stir well for a few minutes.

2. Add the stock and bring to a gentle bubble. Simmer slowly for about 15 minutes, or until all the vegetables are soft, but not mushy!

3. Remove from the heat and allow to cool for 10-15 minutes. Liquidize with a hand blender, adding the cream and cheese as you go.

4. Reheat, taking care not to let the soup boil. Serve in warmed bowls with a good crackle of pepper and the bread rolls.

# 2 Turmeric Butter Chicken with Paratha Breads

This recipe is a bit fiddly and complicated, but it is so worth the effort! I find with recipes like this that it is really important to get yourself prepared so you don't get in a muddle – get your workspace nice and clear, work out what pots and pans you're going to use and measure out your ingredients before you start. Please make sure all your spices are fresh and haven't been sitting in the back of the cupboard for years! We normally have it with a simple salad of tomatoes, onion and cucumber and use the paratha breads to mop all the rich, buttery juices – yum!

*For the Paratha...*

These are best made in advance and reheated when needed...

**300g chapatti flour**
**Pinch of salt**
**50g ghee** (clarified butter)
**150ml lukewarm milk**
**Extra melted ghee and flour for brushing/cooking/rolling/dusting**

1. In a large bowl, mix the salt with the flour. Rub the ghee into the flour with your fingertips, until you have fine crumbs. Make a well in the middle and gradually mix in the milk until you have a firm dough. Turn out onto a floured surface and knead vigorously until smooth, then cover the bowl with a damp tea towel and leave to rest for an hour or so.

2. Divide the dough into 8 portions, then, on a floured surface, roll each one out into 6 inch circles. One at a time, brush with ghee, then dust with flour. Next, fold the disc alternately as if you were making a child's paper fan (ask a friend if you can't remember how to do this!). Stretch it carefully with your fingers, taking care not to snap it, until it's about doubled in length, then on a floured surface coil it tightly like a rope on a ship's deck or a coiled snake and dust with flour.

3. When all your little coils are ready, take one at a time and roll it back flat into a 6 inch disc, then cook in a hot non-stick pan with a little ghee until puffed and browned on both sides.

*For the Chicken...*

## Marinade:

**10 chicken thighs,
skin removed**

**2cm fresh ginger root,
peeled and finely grated**

**50g fresh turmeric root,
skin removed and finely
grated**

**6 cloves of garlic, skin
removed and finely
grated**

**Generous pinch of salt**

**Juice of 1 lemon**

**75ml plain yoghurt**

**2 tbsp garam masala**

## Sauce:

**150g unsalted butter**

**½ onion, very finely
chopped**

**2 cloves garlic, finely
sliced**

**2 cardamom pods**

**3 cloves**

**1 tube tomato puree**

**100ml single cream**

**Juice of 1 lemon**

**2 tsp garam masala**

**1 tbsp chilli flakes**

**1 tbsp nigella seeds**

1. Blend all of the marinade ingredients together and pour over the chicken. Mix well, cover and marinate in the fridge for at least 3 hours, but preferably overnight.

2. Remove the chicken from the marinade and place in a snug-fitting oven dish. Grill it under a hot grill for 15 minutes, turning halfway. Turn the heat off and leave it under the grill to keep warm while you're making the sauce.

3. For the sauce, melt the butter in a saucepan. Add the onion, garlic and spices and sizzle gently for 2-3 minutes, stirring regularly. Add the tomato puree, cream, lemon juice and any left over marinade and stir well. Pour over the chicken and cook in a medium-hot oven for 20 minutes.

*For the Salad...*

**300g aromatic cherry tomatoes, quartered**

**1 red onion, very thinly sliced**

**1 cucumber, cut into thick 'matchsticks'**

**Lemon juice (a good squeeze)**

**Salt and very coarsely ground black pepper**

Mix all the ingredients in a bowl and stir well. Leave for 5 minutes to allow the juices to flow and mingle. Stir well again and serve alongside the chicken and paratha breads.

# 3 Creamy Fish Pie with Potted Brown Shrimp

A good fish pie is hard to beat and this is my favourite way of doing it, with a crispy breadcrumb topping, rather than the usual mashed potato. The addition of brown shrimp gives it that real British *seasidey* taste! Please make sure all fish is bought from a sustainably fished source.

1 small brown onion, thickly sliced

½ fennel bulb, thickly sliced

1 bay leaf

½ leek, chopped

2 garlic cloves, crushed

6 peppercorns

2 cloves

700ml whole milk

300ml single cream

½ tablespoon plain flour

500g smoked haddock fillet, skin removed (keep the skin!)

500g cod loin

Salt and coarsely ground pepper

100g chilled butter

50g potted shrimp

200g white breadcrumbs

Zest of 1 lemon

Extra virgin olive oil

1 bunch flat-leaf parsley, roughly chopped

3 lemons cut into wedges

1. Place the onion, fennel, bay, leek, garlic, peppercorns, cloves, milk, cream and any fish skin into a wide pan and bring to a very gentle simmer. Cook gently for 15 minutes, stirring and squishing occasionally to get the juices flowing. With a slotted spoon, carefully remove all the vegetables, etc. Turn the heat up so your sauce bubbles a bit more vigorously and sieve your flour in, stirring vigorously for a couple of minutes whilst it thickens.

2. Mix your fish, shrimp and lemon zest in a medium size ovenproof dish and season well with salt and pepper.

3. Pour your sauce over the fish mix, cover with the breadcrumbs and grate the chilled butter over the top. Bake at 200°C for 30-35 minutes, or until the top starts to become nice and crispy.

4. Allow to stand uncovered for 10 minutes, before serving in bowls with plenty of fresh parsley and lemon wedges.

# Haggis with Neeps, Tatties and Creamy Onions

I have converted so many people to haggis! It carries a dubious reputation because of its ingredients (basically sheep offal and oats cooked in a stomach), but if you put that out of your mind, then you will find that haggis is one of the most delicious and under-rated dishes there is. Any leftovers are gorgeous for breakfast with eggs and beans. Do try to seek out the best haggis you can get, rather than just a generic supermarket one – it really makes a huge difference!

**1 haggis (approx 750g)**
**4 medium brown onions**
**500ml double cream**
**200g grated farmhouse cheddar**
**500g King Edward potatoes**
**500 turnip or swede**
**100g butter**
**Single malt whisky**

1. Prick the skin of your haggis as you would a baked potato, wrap well in foil and bake in the oven at 180°C for about 1 hour 15 mins. Once the haggis is cooking, make a start on the vegetable dishes.

2. Boil the onions in their skins in a pan of water for about 10-15 minutes or until the tip of a sharp knife passes through them easily. Drain and cool in cold water. When they're cool enough to handle, remove their skins with a sharp knife and arrange them in a snug-fitting ovenproof dish – I usually use a bread tin. Pour over the cream and top with the cheese. Place in a preheated medium-hot oven for 10-15 minutes or until it looks done. Cover with foil and turn the oven down as low as it will go.

3. Boil and mash the potatoes and turnips separately with plenty of butter. Cover and keep warm in the oven if necessary, whilst the haggis finishes cooking.

4. Serve the haggis in warmed bowls with a generous drizzle of whisky and veg on the side.

# Mulato Chile Burritos

Burritos (meaning 'little donkeys', although no one really seems to know why) are a real hands-on, satisfying treat that, when made well, will have you moaning with delicious delight! They originate from Northern Mexico and the Southern US states and this recipe incorporates a lot of traditional flavours from that part of the world, including two types of dried *chiles* (as the Mexicans call chillies) – chipotle and mulato. The chipotle imparts a wonderful smoky flavour, but it's the mulato that takes centre stage in this dish, with flavours of dark chocolate, cherry, licorice and tobacco.

*Beef filling:*

**60g dried mulato chillies**
**40g dried chipotle chillies**
**1 litre boiling water**
**2 tbsp tomato ketchup**
**1 level tbsp Marmite**
**2 tbsp vegetable oil**
**1kg best quality steak mince (not too lean!)**
**2 tsp cumin seeds**
**⅓ stick Mexican cinnamon**
**1 onion, finely chopped**
**6 cloves of garlic, chopped**
**2 tsp dried oregano**
**1tbsp very dark, good quality chocolate, finely grated**
**400g tin black-eyed beans, drained**

*To serve:*

**8 large flour tortillas**
**1 tin pickled jalapeño peppers**
**250g proper farmhouse cheddar, grated**
**Soured cream**
**Guacamole**
**Chopped red onion/tasty tomatoes/crunchy lettuce**

1. Remove the stalks from the dried chillies and shake out the seeds. Chop roughly, then place in a heatproof bowl and cover in the boiling water. Leave for 30 minutes or so to rehydrate. When they have softened up nicely, blend them in a food processor with the infused water, ketchup and Marmite.

2. Heat the oil in a large pan and sizzle the beef on a medium-high heat with a generous sprinkling of salt for about 15 minutes, or until it starts to brown up nicely. Make sure there's plenty of room in the pan, so that the beef mince browns, rather than steams. If you don't have a wide enough pan, then do it in batches.

3. Add the cumin seeds, cinnamon, onion, garlic and oregano and stir for 2-3 minutes.

4. Add your chilli 'stock' and bring to a gentle simmer. Bubble away for 1 hour, topping up with extra water if it looks like it may dry out. After an hour, allow most of the liquid to evaporate away, being VERY careful not to burn it, then stir in the beans and the chocolate for 1 minute. Cover and remove from the heat. Warm the tortillas.

5. Put the chilli pan straight on the table along with all the accoutrements and let everyone create their own delicious burrito!

# 6 Saucisse de Morteau and Potato Roast with Slow Cooked Red Cabbage

Saucisses de Morteau are big, plump, juniper-smoked pork sausages from the Jura mountains of France. In this recipe, the potatoes roast in the fat and gorgeous smoky juices of the sausages and are served with cabbage, slow cooked with apples and lashings of Dijon mustard. Perfect for eating on laps in front of a good film on a wintry Sunday afternoon...

If you're unable to source Morteau sausage, then look for Montbelliard, or a good quality Polish kielbasa.

1 medium red cabbage, thinly shredded

2 medium red onions, thinly sliced

2 large Bramley apples, peeled, cored and thinly sliced

½ cinnamon stick

2 cloves

3 tbsp brown sugar

3 tbsp cider vinegar

75g salted butter

Salt and pepper

500g Morteau sausages, cut into 1 inch chunks

750g floury potatoes, cut into 1 inch cubes

Vegetable oil

Dijon mustard to serve

1. Mix cabbage, onions, apples, cinnamon, cloves, brown sugar, cider vinegar and butter in a suitably sized heavy casserole. Put the lid on and cook oven at 150°C for about 2 hours, stirring once or twice. When the cabbage is done, take it out the oven and leave it somewhere to keep warm.

2. Parboil the potatoes in a large pan. Then drain them, add plenty of salt, put a lid on the pan and give them a good shake so they get a bit 'bashed up'. Next, put a generous glug of oil in a roasting tray and put your tray directly on the hob on a high heat. When it's really hot, carefully add the potatoes. Sizzle them for 4-5 minutes, turning carefully as you go, so they start to crisp up nicely. Add the sausage chunks and pop the tray in the oven at 180°C for 30-35 minutes, or until done, stirring halfway through and basting the potatoes in all the lovely, smoky oil.

3. Serve in bowls with the cabbage and a big dollop of mustard.

# 7 Quick Three Course Valentine's Supper for Two

Nothing says 'I love you' like a romantic home-cooked dinner for two, so instead of taking the easy option and booking an average meal at an average restaurant, score massive brownie points with this impressive but simple three-courser. Make life easier by preparing as much in advance as possible: that way you're not spending all your time in the kitchen!

*FIRST COURSE: Fresh Oysters, with raspberry vinaigrette and Tabasco*

Make the vinaigrette ahead of time so all you need to do is shuck and serve.

**6 fresh oysters**
**50ml raspberry vinegar**
**Handful of raspberries**
**1 large purple shallot, chopped very finely**
**Tabasco sauce (optional)**
**Bread and butter**
**You will also need some crushed ice (or smash some ice cubes in a tea towel with a rolling pin)**

1. Set aside 6 raspberries and then add the rest, along with the shallots, to the vinegar. Mix well, and crush with a fork to get all the juices flowing. Leave for at least 30 minutes, stirring occasionally. This can be made ahead of time and stored in the fridge.

2. Carefully shuck the oysters and sit them on a bed of ice. Add a teaspoon of vinaigrette to each and garnish with the leftover raspberries. Serve with the buttered bread and optional Tabasco.

## SECOND COURSE: Baked heart-shaped Neufchâtel cheese with onion confit

You can prepare the bread ahead of time so all you need to do is pop it all in the oven!

**1 Neufchâtel heart-shaped cheese**

**Splash of white wine**

**1 jar onion confit/onion marmalade**

**½ baguette, cut into largish bite-sized pieces**

**1 tsp red chilli flakes**

**1 clove garlic, crushed**

**1 sprig of rosemary, leaves removed and finely chopped**

**Lashings of extra virgin olive oil**

1. Preheat the oven to 180°C. Put the cheese in a snug-fitting ovenproof ramekin or dish and add a splash of white wine. Cook for 20 minutes, or until it goes soft and gooey.

2. While the cheese is cooking, toss the bread, chilli flakes, garlic, rosemary and oil together in a bowl. You can do this earlier in the day, cover or place in a food bag and set aside until needed. Transfer to an oven tray and bake, turning occasionally, until starting to crisp up. This should take no more than 10 minutes.

3. Put your onion confit into a serving dish and your bread bites into a bowl, serve the cheese hot out of the oven and use forks to dip the bread into the cheese. Top with a dollop of onion confit, or pile the confit on top of the cheese, before digging in.

## THIRD COURSE: Molten chocolate teacups with passion fruit cream

It's a good idea to get these prepped up first, before you start on the other courses, so they're ready to go...

### For the passion fruit cream...

**1 egg yolk**

**2 tbsp caster sugar**

**1 tbsp Cointreau or Triple Sec**

**3 passion fruits, flesh and seeds removed**

**100ml double cream**

1. Whisk the egg yolk and sugar together vigorously for 2-3 minutes, until it's lovely and light and fluffy, then beat in the Cointreau/Triple Sec and passion fruit. Next, in a separate bowl whip the cream until it stiffens a bit and fold in the egg mix. Chill in the fridge until you're ready to serve.

*For the chocolate teacups...*

NB The proportions used are quite generous to account for different sized teacups, so don't worry if there's some mix left over. You can always make up more and store them in the fridge; they can be frozen too. Extra sauce can be kept in a sterilised jar and is great warmed up over ice cream or with raspberry tart, berries and meringue, pancakes, etc. Also, it can be used to make rice crispy cakes!

*For the pudding:*

**100g bar very good quality dark chocolate**
**100g caster sugar**
**50g unsalted butter, softened**
**80g self raising flour**
**2 eggs, beaten**

*For the sauce:*

**25g caster sugar**
**50g butter**
**2 tbsp golden syrup**
**25g cocoa powder**

1. Break the chocolate into a glass bowl. Microwave on medium-high for about 30 seconds, until the pieces have nearly fully melted, but with still a little bit of wet-firmness in the middle. Mix in the sugar and softened butter with a silicone spatula and stir well – there should be enough heat left in the chocolate to melt it all into a smooth sauce. Sift in the flour and mix well again. Lastly, whisk in the eggs until smooth.

2. Make the sauce: put all the ingredients together in a small saucepan and bring together over a low heat.

3. Butter 2 large teacups (or 4 small), put a good couple of tablespoons of sauce in the bottom of each, then fill with your pudding mixture to just over halfway (they will rise a lot). Cover and set aside in the fridge until you're ready to heat them up. These can be stored for up to a week.

4. When you're ready, microwave on full for about a minute, then either eat out of the cups or turn out onto plates for the full oozy dramatic effect. Serve with a generous dollop of the passion fruit cream.

# Russian Morel Chicken

The unique flavour and unusual honeycomb appearance of morel mushrooms makes them prized by cooks all over the world. In the UK they emerge any time from late March to May. Notoriously difficult to find, they command a high price, but are worth every penny. If you can't get hold of fresh morels, then substitute with rehydrated dried ones. Russian cuisine values mushrooms perhaps more than any other and this recipe is in a traditional Russian style, with a very rich, creamy morel sauce, amplified with a lot of sherry!

**750g Maris Piper potatoes**
**Salted butter**
**4 free-range chicken breasts**
**1 tbsp plain flour**
**Salt and black pepper**
**Olive oil**
**200g fresh morel mushrooms**
**30g dried porcini mushrooms**
**500ml dry sherry**
**500ml good quality chicken stock**
**100ml double cream**
**50g butter**
**2 small red onions, cut into rings**
**200g flaked Parmesan cheese**
**100g fresh rocket**

1. Slice your potatoes, then boil and mash with a good knob of butter, so they're nice and creamy. Put them in a snug ovenproof dish. Cover with foil and keep warm in a low oven.

2. Put the dried porcini mushrooms in a small jug and add a pint of boiling water.

3. Dust the chicken breasts with the flour and season well. Heat a glug of oil in a large pan and brown them off well on both sides (5-10 minutes). Add the sherry and bubble vigorously for 5 minutes, then add the chicken stock and the porcini (with its water). Bring to a steady simmer and bubble for 30-40 minutes or until the liquid has reduced by at least half, turning the chicken occasionally. Stir in the cream and simmer for another 5 minutes, or until you have a beautiful silky sauce. Cover the pan with a lid and remove from the heat.

4. Fry the onions in batches, on a high heat with plenty of salt and coarsely ground black pepper until crispy and caramelised. (If you try and do them all in one go, they're likely to steam a bit and not go crispy!) Remove from the pan and set aside, uncovered. Turn the heat down a little and add the morels to the pan for 4-5 minutes or until they're cooked (depending on the size of the morels).

5. To serve, put a neat round bed of mash on each warmed plate. Top with the chicken, then the parmesan, rocket, onion and morels, in as neat a little tower as you can. Finish by pouring the sauce carefully around your little stacks, wiping off any splashes with a cloth as you go.

# 9 Smoked Eel with Beetroot and Horseradish Salsa

The construction of the magnificent Ely Cathedral in the 11th century was largely funded by the sale of eels – showing how highly valued a delicacy they once were. Eel has a unique, rich, yet delicate flavour that's not too 'fishy' and a soft, oily texture. Unfortunately, due to over-fishing and loss of habitat, the humble eel was brought almost to the brink of extinction in the UK, but now, thanks to huge conservation efforts, they are making a comeback; but please still ensure that you only buy eels from a sustainable source.

300g smoked eel fillets, cut into pieces large enough to nearly cover a slice of baguette

4 small cooked beetroot (not in vinegar), chopped small

2 pickled gherkins, chopped small

½ small onion, very finely chopped

2 tbsp horseradish sauce

Coarsely ground black pepper

Good quality baguette, cut into slices

Salted butter

Butter your bread and top with horseradish, then eel, beetroot, dill pickles, onion and a sprig of dill.

# 10 Tartiflette

Tartiflette is a classic dish from the Savoie region of France, made from pungent Reblochon cheese, potatoes and bacon. If anyone claims that any other meal is the 'ultimate comfort food', they are wrong. THIS is the ultimate comfort food...

When selecting your cheese, if possible look for a *fermier* Reblochon, with a green dot on the rind. This will be a proper farmhouse cheese made from raw milk and will be the most flavoursome.

**1kg waxy potatoes, such as Katy**

**1 large onion, sliced**

**300g thick cut smoked bacon, cut into lardons**

**4 garlic cloves, finely chopped**

**300ml crème fraîche**

**Reblochon cheese, preferably *fermier***

**Green salad and balsamic vinegar to serve**

1. Turn the oven on low and warm a suitably sized ovenproof dish – a smallish lasagne dish is perfect.

2. Parboil the potatoes until they're just starting to soften. Drain and set aside

3. Sizzle up the onions with the lardons for about 5 minutes, or until nicely browned. Add the garlic for 30 seconds, then tip into your cooking dish, along with the potatoes and mix well. Pour over the crème fraîche.

4. Slice the Reblochon horizontally along its middle, so you have 2 thin discs, then in half again, so you have 4 half-moons. Arrange them on top of your potato mix, skin side up, and bake at 180°C for about half an hour, or until crispy on top.

5. Serve with salad and balsamic vinegar.

# 11 Fabada Asturiana

Fabada is a traditional dish from the Spanish province of Asturias. It's a really hearty meal, consisting of beans and pork done in about every which way imaginable! My recipe includes chorizo, bacon and Morcilla (Spanish black pudding).

**500g dried *fabes* or butter beans, soaked overnight in plenty of cold water (use bottled water if you live in a hard water area)**

**250g cooking chorizo, cut into 2cm thick rings**

**250g Morcilla, cut into 2cm thick rings**

**150g thick cut unsmoked streaky bacon, cut into short strips**

**Pinch of saffron**

**1 bay leaf**

1. Drain the soaked beans and place in a large, wide pan. Cover by a couple of centimetres with hot water and bring to a fairly vigorous simmer. Let them cook for 10 minutes, stirring as you go and skimming off any scum that forms on the water.

2. Turn the heat down to a slow simmer and add the rest of the ingredients, then cook for about 2½ hours or until the beans are soft. During the cooking process, keep the water level topped up as you go so it doesn't dry out.

3. Once the beans are cooked, taste and adjust the seasoning. Put a lid on the pot and leave it to stand for a good 10-15 minutes before serving.

# 12 Homemade Bangers and Brown Sauce

I love making sausages so much and it really is so easy. To begin with you don't even need any fancy equipment (although I do heartily recommend investing in a sausage maker if you're going to make them regularly). All you need is a wide-necked funnel and wooden spoon or rolling pin. Most butchers will oblige you with a length of casing if you buy your meat from them. For me, nothing compliments a good banger like brown sauce, so while you're at it, why not make your own? This recipe should make a litre or more, so store any leftovers in sterilised bottles/jars.

*For the sausages...*

**2 metres of sausage casing**

**500g free-range pork shoulder, minced**

**250g free-range pork belly, minced**

**25g fine dried breadcrumbs**

**½ tsp white pepper**

**1 tsp black pepper**

**1 tbsp fresh rosemary, very finely chopped**

**2 tbsp fresh parsley, finely chopped**

**2 tbsp wholegrain mustard**

**1 tsp salt**

1. Put the sausage skin in a sink of cold water. Leave it for half an hour, then drain the sink. Find one end and carefully put it under the running tap, so the skin gets rinsed inside and out and generally stretched and loosened a bit.

2. Mix all the other ingredients together well in a large bowl. Fry off a little bit of your mixture in a pan and taste it, so you can adjust the seasoning, etc., if need be.

3. To fill your sausages, run your finger and thumb down the skin to squeeze out any excess water, then hitch it all up onto the spout of your clean funnel, with a few inches overhanging the end.

4. Start pushing your mixture into the funnel, using the end of a rolling pin, or wooden spoon. Once the meat starts filling the casing, tie the end off with some string, then keep filling until you've used all your sausage meat. Careful not to pack it too tightly, and don't worry if its a bit uneven – it will still taste just as good!

5. Now you need to make your individual sausages. Start at the tied end and carefully pinch and twist your sausage lengths. Then, find the middle of the string and fold it in half on your work surface. Twist together pairs of sausages until you get to the end, then tie and snip off any excess casing. Put on a plate and leave overnight in the fridge, uncovered.

*For the brown sauce...*

**2 onions, chopped**
**500g Bramley apples,**
  **peeled, cored and cut**
  **into chunks**
**1 tin chopped tomatoes**
**200g dark molasses**
**3 cloves of garlic, minced**
**200g pitted dates**
**50g caster sugar**
**100ml Worcester sauce**
**500ml cider vinegar**
**200ml water**
**1 tbsp black pepper**
**2cm fresh ginger root,**
  **finely grated**
**½ tsp ground cinnamon**
**½ tsp ground clove**
**1 tsp Cayenne pepper**

1. Place all the ingredients in a large pan and cover. Bring to a gentle boil and simmer for 1 hour.

2. Whizz it all up in the pan with a hand blender until smooth and simmer again, this time with the lid off, for another half an hour or so, or until it is a nice saucy consistency. Pour into sterilised jars and allow to cool overnight

3. When you're ready to eat them, sizzle up the sausages and serve with your brown sauce and some lovely creamy mash.

# 13 Very Tomatoey and Garlicky Chicken with Parmesan Potato Gratin

This amazing dish shows that recipes don't have to be complicated to be absolutely delicious! All that's needed here is good quality ingredients and a bit of care. You want to really cook this slow and long until you are left with a very thick, rich tomato sauce.

**8-12 free-range chicken thighs**

**3 tins of best quality chopped tomatoes (preferably San Marzano)**

**8 garlic cloves, chopped**

**2 quarters of a fresh lemon**

**1 tbsp extra virgin olive oil**

**Salt and pepper**

**1kg King Edward potatoes, peeled and sliced very thinly – about 3-4mm**

**100g freshly grated Parmesan cheese**

**2 cloves of garlic, crushed**

**2 bay leaves**

**1 sprig of rosemary**

**300ml double cream**

**300ml full fat milk**

1. Heat the olive oil in a large flat pan. Season the chicken thighs with salt and pepper and sizzle at a good heat until both sides are well browned.

2. Add the tomatoes, garlic and lemon, turn down the heat and bring to a gentle bubble. Season well with salt and pepper. Simmer slowly, uncovered, for about 1½ hours or until almost all the liquid has gone. This needs to be a slow process so be patient and keep the heat nice and low. Stir it regularly, and make sure that the sauce doesn't stick and burn.

3. Once the chicken is underway, pour the milk and cream into a large pan and stir well. Add the garlic, bay, rosemary and potatoes. Bring to a gentle boil and simmer for 4-5 minutes.

4. Butter an ovenproof dish and transfer half the contents of your pan, followed by half the Parmesan, then the other half and sprinkle the rest of the cheese on top.

5. Heat the oven to 200°C. Cover your dish with foil and bake for 45 minutes.

6. Remove from the oven. With a dinner knife, check the potatoes are cooked and soft. If they're done, then remove the foil and bake for a further 10 minutes or so, until the top browns up nicely.

# 14 Indian Style Mutton Meatballs in a Tomato Sauce, with Nigella Cauliflower Rice

There are loads of really mouth-watering, powerful flavours going on in this recipe and the cauliflower makes a lovely alternative to boring old rice! If you can find mutton, then use it, but otherwise lamb is fine.

1kg mutton or goat mince (or lamb if they are unavailable)

1 cup grated fresh coconut

2 tbsp fresh yoghurt

1 tbsp garam masala

2 green chillies, deseeded and chopped

Vegetable oil

1 big cauliflower, leaves removed and florets separated

1 tbsp nigella seeds

Large knob of butter

1 tbsp cumin seed

2 tins good-quality chopped tomatoes

1 cm fresh ginger root, minced

Juice of half a lemon

1 tsp ground turmeric

½ tsp ground cinnamon

25g fresh coriander, chopped

2 garlic cloves, minced

1. In a large bowl, mix the mutton, coconut, yoghurt, garam masala and chillies together. Cover and marinate for a couple of hours.

2. Pass the cauliflower through the grating blade of a food processor, so it separates into rice-size pieces. Stir in the nigella, put a large nob of butter on top and put it in a microwaveable dish with a lid.

3. Once marinated, form the meatballs in your hands (oil your hands to stop them sticking too much) then sizzle them in vegetable oil, on a medium heat, until they're nicely browned. Remove from the pan and set aside somewhere warm.

4. Add the cumin seeds to your meatball pan and stir for a minute, then add the tomatoes, ginger, lemon juice, turmeric and cinnamon. Bring to the boil and simmer and reduce gently for 15-20 minutes, mashing the tomato with a spoon as you go to make the sauce smoother.

5. Put the meatballs back in the pan with the sauce, add the fresh garlic and fresh coriander and stir for 1 minute, then remove from the heat.

6. Microwave the cauliflower on full power for 1 minute, with a lid on. Take it out and stir it, then back in for another minute or until it's softened up, and serve.

# 15 English Farmhouse Cheese and Pork Pie Ploughman's

This meal is more of an exercise in shopping than of preparing food yourself, so take the time to seek out the very best ingredients you can! There has been such a resurgence in British cheeses over the past decade or so that there is now so much choice – the cheeses listed below are just suggestions and if you can't find them, substitute with whatever you can find in your local specialist food shop. Look for real farmhouse cheeses, preferably made with raw milk; try and avoid anything that comes pre-packaged in plastic or wax! You want different styles (hard, blue, soft) and different milks (cow, goat, sheep). Likewise, if you can't find any pork pies that appeal (a bad pork pie can be a very depressing experience), then substitute with a good cooked ham.

**200g Cheddar Gorge Cheddar cheese**
**200g Colston Bassett Shropshire Blue cheese**
**200g Baron Bigod cheese**
**1 Dorstone Goat cheese**
**1 large pork pie**
**1 jar of piccalilli**
**1 bunch spring onions**
**4 sticks celery**
**A selection of fruit – apples, pears and grapes are a good bet**
**Nice crusty bread and a selection of cheese biscuits**

Arrange all of the ingredients on the table as nicely as you can and let everyone help themselves.

49

# 16 Spice Fried Fish with Yoghurt and Lavash Flatbreads

Be prepared for watery eyes and a VERY smoky kitchen – countless times I've set off the smoke alarm making this, so it's extractor fans on max and windows open wide!

On the plus side, this recipe is quick, simple and delicious and great fun to make-perfect for an evening with friends.

We used to make this a lot when we lived in the Caribbean and used kingfish or wahoo. They can be tricky to get hold of in the UK, but any other meaty, solid fish such as swordfish or tuna work just as well! Lavash is a soft, thin, unleavened type of flatbread, popular in the Caucasus and Middle East. If it's unavailable to you, then try to use the thinnest flatbreads you can find. You want it to be a vehicle for the delicious fish, rather than a main feature!

1kg meaty fish steaks
3 tbsp garam masala
1 tbsp chilli flakes
1 tbsp ground turmeric
1 tbsp cumin seeds
2 cloves garlic, chopped
Salt and pepper
500ml full fat yoghurt
1 large red onion, cut into rings
2 lemons, cut into wedges
2 limes, cut into wedges
6 ripe vine tomatoes, in wedges
1 bunch coriander, chopped
Lavash flatbread
Vegetable oil for frying

1. Cut the fish into bite-sized chunks. Pat dry with kitchen towel, then cover well with the spices and garlic and plenty of salt and pepper (add more spices if you need to).

2. Heat a small glug of oil in a large, flat pan so it's nice and hot. Fry the fish in batches, ensuring that there's plenty of room in the pan so it doesn't steam, and that each batch goes into hot oil.

3. Toss the coriander with the tomatoes and lay everything out so people can help themselves.

# 17 St George's Mushroom and Wild Garlic Rillettes

The St George's mushroom is a strongly flavoured, meaty mushroom, that appears on grassland and woodland edges around the end of April through to the beginning of June. At the same time, wild garlic plants, or ramsons, are filling our deciduous woodlands with their cheery white flowers and heady aroma! Flavour-wise, these two are a match made in heaven and here, they're combined with a splash of Marsala to make a simple pâté that's delicious on toast as a light, spring-time supper.

**250g butter**

**400g St George's mushrooms (or button mushrooms)**

**Marsala wine**

**50g wild garlic (ramson) leaves**

**Juice of 1 lemon**

**Salt and coarsely ground black pepper**

1. Rinse the mushrooms thoroughly, then place on a cake cooling rack in a warm, dry spot. Leave for a couple of days, so they can air-dry a bit, helping the flavours to intensify.

2. Chop the mushrooms as finely as you can and then roughly chop the wild garlic. Heat up a large frying pan and sizzle them up in about a quarter of the butter for 3-4 minutes, until it all starts to soften. Add a generous glug of Marsala, the lemon juice and plenty of salt and pepper and bubble for another 5 minutes or so, so that most of the liquid evaporates.

3. Turn down the heat and slowly melt in the rest of the butter. Pack into a suitably sized jar and chill in the fridge for a minimum of 2 hours, but preferably overnight.

4. Serve with hot toast.

# 18 Spicy Italian Sausage and Buffalo Mozzarella Penne Pasta

This recipe is quick, easy and absolutely delicious, but beware: poor quality ingredients have nowhere to hide when you're making dishes this simple, so please ensure you get the absolute best pasta you can find and only use buffalo milk Mozzarella. The best way to select tomatoes is to smell them – they should be pungent and aromatic. Your olive oil should be cold-pressed extra virgin and the balsamic aged, thick and gloopy. Needless to say, as the focal point of the meal, your sausages should be really top drawer; but as you can't usually taste or smell them before buying, I find a good tip is to look at the packaging and the price. Sausages with a great long list of suspicious sounding ingredients (usually preservatives, etc.) should be avoided; remember that if the sausages come cheap, then they'll probably taste cheap too!

500g spicy Italian sausages, cut into 2cm chunks

2 medium red onions, cut into 8

1 tsp fennel seeds

2 fresh buffalo Mozzarella balls, torn roughly into eighths and drained of excess water

300g best quality penne pasta

150g Parmigiano Reggiano, finely grated

100g fresh rocket

200g aromatic baby plum tomatoes, cut in half

Extra virgin olive oil

Thick and gloopy balsamic vinegar

1. Cook the pasta *al dente*, strain and set aside.

2. Add a good glug of olive oil to a large pan. Add the sausage and onions and sizzle on a medium-high heat until the onion is starting to caramelise and the sausages are nicely browned. Add the fennel seeds and stir for a minute.

3. Turn the heat down a bit and add the pasta. Stir for a couple of minutes, then add the tomatoes and stir for 1 more minute: the tomatoes should be warmed and softening a bit but not completely cooked. Next, stir in the Mozzarella for 30 seconds, then the rocket and Parmesan. Turn the heat off, put the lid on and leave to stand for 5 minutes.

4. Serve in warmed bowls with a goodly drizzle of balsamic and olive oil!

# 19 Soft-Boiled Goose Eggs with Asparagus Soldiers

These two fantastic ingredients start to appear in the shops and farmers' markets at the same time, so it would seem churlish not to serve them together. My kids love this recipe and would eat it every day if they could!

4 fresh goose eggs
2 bunches British asparagus
Thick sliced granary bread, butter and Marmite

1. Get 2 large pans of boiling water on the go – one for the eggs and one for the asparagus.

2. Cook the eggs for 7 minutes and the asparagus for 3-6 minutes, depending on the thickness of the stalks.

3. Use the asparagus to dip into the eggs and serve with plenty of buttered toast and Marmite.

# 20 Messy Crayfish Feast with Spicy Ali-Oli Dip

One evening, several years ago, a friend of mine came bursting in, practically exploding with excitement... 'Check it out!' he said triumphantly, emptying out a rucksack full of live crayfish into my kitchen sink! He subsequently explained to his bemused audience that he'd been out fishing; with not much biting, he had taken to luring out the voracious little crustaceans with his bacon sandwiches and scooping them up with a landing net. What followed was one of the most fun, delicious, and messiest feasts I think I've ever had... cracking open shells with whatever we had at hand – pliers, adjustable spanners and a hammer!

Of course, you are unlikely to have such a ready supply of fresh crayfish, but they are available to buy online precooked and frozen, so all you need to do is reheat in boiling water.

**4 dozen pre-cooked frozen whole crayfish**

**300g mayonnaise**

**4 large cloves of garlic, minced**

**Juice of 1 lemon**

**1 heaped tsp dried chilli flakes**

**1 heaped tbsp finely chopped flat leaf parsley**

**Bread and butter to serve**

1. Mix all the dip ingredients together in a bowl, cover and set aside in the fridge.

2. Get a big pan of water on the boil. Drop in the crayfish, bring back to the boil and cook for 10 minutes, or as per cooking instructions for pre-cooked crayfish. Drain them off and serve on a big platter with the alioli and bread on the side. Make sure you've lots of napkins, a bits-bowl and plenty of tools, then get cracking!

# 21 Beef Rendang

Beef Rendang is a South-East Asian curry, in which the beef is slow-cooked in aromatic spices and coconut milk until it is melt-in-the-mouth tender and exploding with exotic flavours.

I've spent years perfecting the spice combination in this, which is one of my all-time favourite dishes!

2 red onions, peeled and roughly chopped

2 stalks lemongrass, outer leaves removed and roughly chopped

6 garlic cloves, peeled

2cm root ginger, peeled and roughly chopped

75g galangal, peeled and roughly chopped

4 large red, mild chillies (you're going for a fruity spice, not a brutal burn!), roughly chopped

Vegetable oil

3 star anise

2 cardamom pods

2 cloves

4-5 Kaffir lime leaves

1 kg braising steak, cut into chunks

1 400ml can coconut milk

1 generous tbsp tamarind paste

1 tbsp soft brown sugar

1 tsp salt

Steamed Jasmine rice to serve

1. In a food processor, blend the onions, lemongrass, garlic, ginger, galangal and chillies with 2 tbsp vegetable oil, until you have a smooth paste.,

2. Heat the remaining oil in a large, flat-bottomed pan and add the meat. Stir for a couple of minutes, then add the spice paste and brown gently for 4-5 minutes, stirring constantly.

3. Pour in the coconut milk, fill the empty can with water, give it a swirl and pour that in too. Stir in the tamarind, sugar and salt and add the remaining spices and lime leaves.

4. Bring to a gentle bubble, and cook slowly for about 2 hours, or until almost all the liquid has gone and you have a very thick, rich sauce. Be careful towards the end that it doesn't dry out and burn!

5. Serve in bowls with steamed Jasmine rice.

# 22 Lovage Chicken Stew

We have a lovage plant in our garden that every year grows to monstrous proportions! Like most people, at first I didn't have a clue what to do with this underused herb, which tastes like a heady mix of celery, parsley, curry and aniseed. However, after lots of trial and error, we came up with some wonderful recipes, but it is this lovely simple chicken stew that we come back to again and again...

8 free-range chicken thighs, skin removed and cut in half across the bone with a cleaver or heavy knife (NB keep the chicken skins in the freezer for later use)

100g fresh lovage leaves and stems, chopped

2 sticks celery, chopped

1 big carrot, cut into thick slices

1 tsp dried mixed peppercorns

6 garlic cloves, sliced thinly

2 onions, peeled and sliced

2 tbsp extra virgin olive oil

1 handful mixed olives with stones – we use lucques, tanches and arbequina

1 tin best-quality chopped plum tomatoes

500g small new potatoes

Crusty bread and butter to serve

1. Heat the oil in a large pot and sizzle the chicken for 4-5 minutes.

2. Add all the other ingredients, except the potatoes. Bring to the boil and simmer gently for 30 minutes with a lid on.

3. Remove the lid and continue to simmer gently for another 1½ hours or so, or until the liquid has reduced by about a third.

4. Add the potatoes and cook until they're soft, but not mushy!

5. Serve in bowls with crusty bread and butter.

# 23 Jewelled Tabbouleh with Fresh Houmous

This is a spectacular looking, nourishing dish, with lots of refreshing, zingy flavours and juicy textures. At home, it's our go-to meal, for when we want a meal that feels super healthy, without being dull! Home-made houmous is so easy to make and *soooo* much nicer than your average shop-bought equivalent.

## Tabbouleh:

300g bulgar wheat, rehydrated in boiling water and well drained
1 red onion, finely chopped
2 garlic cloves, minced
Juice of 1 lemon
50g flat leaf parsley, coarsely chopped
25g fresh mint, chopped.
1 handful of mixed olives, pitted (NB Please don't use pitted olives. Buy stone-in ones and pit them yourself. The taste is completely different!)
Coarsely ground black pepper
10 medjool dates, seeded and roughly chopped
100g pomegranate seeds
50ml extra virgin olive oil

## Houmous:

2 cans chickpeas in brine, drained
Juice of 2 lemons, plus extra to taste
5 garlic cloves, minced
250ml tahini
100ml extra virgin olive oil, plus extra to taste
1 tbsp cumin seeds
Crusty bread to serve (optional)

## Directions for Tabbouleh

Mix all the ingredients together in a bowl. Stir well, cover and set aside in the fridge whilst you make the houmous, stirring occasionally to let the flavours mingle.

## Directions for Houmous

1. Blend all the ingredients together in a food processor until smooth. Taste and add more lemon juice or olive oil if required.

2. Heat a tablespoon of olive oil in a small pan. Toast the cumin seeds for a minute or so, until browned and aromatic and stir into the houmous. Serve immediately with your tabbouleh and bread if you're having it.

# 24 Mediterranean Oven Baked Tuna with Oregano Tomatoes and Olives

Every springtime we go on a pilgrimage to the Greek Island of Lesvos to watch the annual bird migration. By the time we get there, there are already plenty of wonderfully flavoured tomatoes available, and the hillsides are covered in pungent-smelling oregano, which is just bursting into flower. This recipe is a very simple, typical way of preparing wonderful fresh fish. Serve the fish whole on a platter, slicing as you go and with a big bowl of thin, crispy chips and plenty of bread to mop up the wonderful juices!

1kg tuna loin
4 cloves of garlic, sliced
750g fresh plum tomatoes, cut in half, seeds scooped out
1 large red onion, sliced thinly
1 tsp good quality dried oregano
Handful mixed, stone-in olives
½ small glass of dry white wine
Extra virgin olive oil
750g King Edward potatoes
1 litre olive pomace oil

1. Cut your potatoes, skins and all, into matchsticks. Place in a large bowl of cold water and allow to soak, to remove some excess starch.

2. Preheat the oven to 200°C. Season the tuna fillet generously with salt and pepper and sear it off in a hot pan with a splash of oil, along with the onion for 4-5 minutes. If it sticks at any point, don't try and pull it off, just leave it and it will unstick itself.

3. Transfer the tuna to a roasting tray, scattering the tomatoes, garlic, oregano and olives around it. Drizzle the tomatoes with oil and pour the wine over the fish and bake, uncovered, for about 20 minutes. Once cooked, let it rest whist you're making the chips.

4. Drain your potato chips well and heat the oil in a large pan on the hob. Test when the oil is hot enough by dropping a chip in it and see if it sizzles: if it sizzles very aggressively, then turn it down a notch. Cook the chips (in batches if necessary) and pile into a bowl on a bit of kitchen roll.

5. Slice the fish thinly at the table, pour over the tomatoes and any juices, and let everyone help themselves to chips.

# 25 Prosciutto San Daniele, Burrata and Strawberry Salad

Burrata – meaning 'buttered' in Italian – is a fresh Mozzarella-style cheese from Puglia, with an unctuous, creamy rich centre. In this recipe it combines beautifully with fresh strawberries, prosciutto and aromatic basil. There is a real glut of strawberries at this time of year, but sadly so many of them are 'grown for the shelves': in other words, they look good, last for ages, but have very little flavour! Try and seek out some different varieties to the ubiquitous Elsanta. In fact, why not go the whole hog and pick your own – that way you can ensure the pick of the crop! My favourite Italian ham is San Daniele which has a sweeter, more delicate flavour than Prosciutto di Parma, but either works well.

**50g fresh basil leaves**

**16 very thin slices prosciutto San Daniele**

**100g burrata**

**300g strawberries, hulled and cut in half**

**Thick and sweet balsamic vinegar**

**Extra virgin olive oil**

**Coarsely ground black pepper**

**Crusty bread to serve**

On each plate, place a burrata on a bed of basil leaves, and then carefully arrange the other ingredients around it. Drizzle with olive oil and balsamic vinegar and a good crackle of black pepper.

Serve with crusty bread on the side.

# 26 Pork Chops with Gooseberry Sauce and Creamy Mash

Gooseberries are one of those ingredients that you see everywhere in the summer, but which, besides the obvious crumble or pie, you don't really know what to do with. A friend once cooked something similar to this for me and it turns out that gooseberries and pork are a match made in heaven!

4 nice fat pork chops
2 tbsp olive oil
200g fresh gooseberries
8 sprigs of thyme
200ml medium-sweet cider or apple juice
1 heaped tbsp brown sugar
Salted butter
750g floury potatoes, such as King Edward, peeled and thickly sliced

1. Bring a pan of water to the boil and cook the potatoes until soft, but not mushy. Add a couple of goodly knobs of butter and mash until smooth and creamy. Put a lid on the pan and set aside somewhere warmish.

2. Heat the olive oil in a pan and fry the pork chops for 4-5 minutes on each side – not forgetting the rind!

3. Add the gooseberries, thyme, cider, sugar and a good knob of butter and bubble fairly vigorously for 2-3 minutes, until the gooseberries have softened and the sauce has reduced a bit. Serve on warmed plates with a generous dollop of mash.

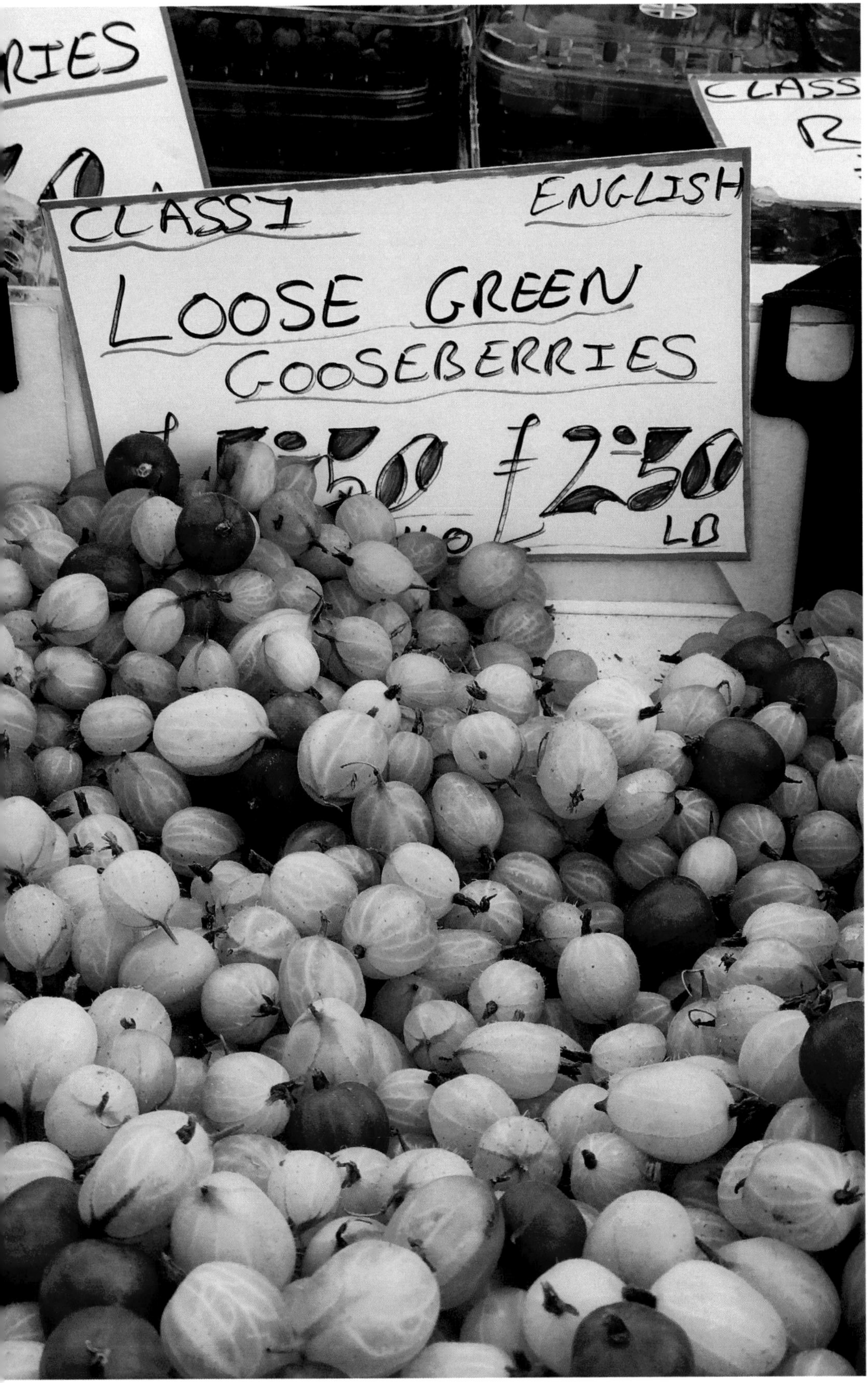
CLASS1
ENGLISH
LOOSE GREEN
GOOSEBERRIES
£2.50
LB

# 27 Cream Tea with Rose Petal Jam

Imagine white fluffy clouds overhead, the sound of singing skylarks, the chink of fine bone china and the heady smell of roses in the warm summer sunshine... Ahhhh, what could be better? This recipe uses fresh rose petals to make an incredibly fragrantly flavoured jam that goes beautifully with home made scones and lashings of clotted cream

*For the jam...*

**70g fresh, aromatic rose petals, all the same colour**
**800ml water**
**400g jam sugar**

1. Rinse off the rose petals to get rid of any dirt or bugs, then place them in a bowl and cover with water. Place another bowl over the top and weigh down so that all the petals are immersed. Leave overnight.

2. Drain the petals from the rose water which should now have a slight blush to it and smell fragrant and rosy. Set the water aside. Sprinkle some sugar over the rose petals and mix together, bruising the leaves as you do so. Leave to macerate for an hour or so, even overnight again if you have the time.

3. Add the rose water and jam sugar to a large saucepan over a high heat. Once the sugar has melted, add the rose petals and turn the heat to medium. Leave to simmer gently for 20 minutes or so. If you have a jam thermometer, set it in the pan and wait for it to reach the desired heat. Otherwise, put a plate in the freezer and test the jam by putting a spoonful on the chilled plate. Slowly run your finger through it and if it wrinkles as you do so and stays separate rather than running back together, then the jam is set.

4. Spoon into sterilised jars and seal quickly. This recipe makes about two 1lb jars and it will keep for many months.

*For the scones...*

**250g plain flour**
**1 tsp bicarbonate of soda**
**2tsp cream of tartar**
**65g salted butter, cubed and chilled**
**25g caster sugar**
**150ml whole milk**
**1 free-range egg, beaten**
**Plenty of clotted cream and a top-quality leaf tea to serve**

1. Pre-heat the oven to 220°C. Mix the flour, bicarbonate and cream of tartar in a large bowl, then rub in the butter with your fingers until it's like fine breadcrumbs. Don't over-work the butter! Stir in the sugar, then slowly add the milk using just enough so that it comes together into a dough.

2. Take the rough dough out of the bowl and bring it together quickly with your hands (not too much!) on a floured surface.

3. Flat the dough out with your hands so it's about 4cm deep, then cut out the scones with a cutter and arrange them on a greased baking sheet. Beat the remaining milk with the egg and glaze. Bake for 12 minutes or until well risen and golden.

4. Get out your best china and serve the scones warm with lashings of clotted cream, jam and pots of tea!

# 28 BBQ Sea Trout with Fresh Samphire, Lemon and Garlic Butter

Summertime for me means samphire. Growing up on the back of a salt marsh in Norfolk, we used to go out picking in our wellies and come back sunburned and covered from head to toe in smelly black mud! Luckily, samphire is much easier to come by these days and most fishmongers will have it in when it's in season. At the same time the samphire is growing, my favourite fish in the world comes into its oh-too-short season. Sea trout are migratory brown trout. They more closely resemble salmon than freshwater trout, but, in my opinion, taste better than either! If you can't get hold of sea trout, just about any fish will work here, as long as it's whole and fresh.

**1 large sea trout, about 1.5kg in weight, gutted and scaled**
**½ block of butter**
**6 lemons, cut into wedges**
**6 cloves of garlic, minced**
**500g fresh samphire, well rinsed**
**Plenty of crusty bread and butter**

1. Beat the butter in a small bowl with a fork until it softens, then mix in the minced garlic.

2. With a sharp knife, slash the fish on both sides, every 3 inches or so down its length. Drizzle all over with olive oil and salt generously.

3. Light the BBQ and when it's settled down to a medium heat, use tongs to oil the grill with a clean rag soaked in olive oil. Cook the fish for about 10-15 minutes on each side, depending on its thickness. A general rule of thumb is ten minutes of total cooking time per inch of thickness (at the thickest part of the fish).

4. Bring a pot of water to the boil and drop the rinsed samphire in it. Cook for a couple of minutes then drain.

5. Serve the fish whole on a large platter with the samphire and lemon wedges and smothered in the garlic butter. Give everyone a plate and cutlery, loads of crusty bread, black pepper, plenty of clean napkins, a bits-bowl for any fish bones and samphire stalks and get stuck in.

# 29 Minted Feta Salad with Nectarines and Raspberries

This is a wonderfully vibrant summer salad. It's crucial that the nectarines are ripe and juicy; that you use a good Feta, preferably made from sheeps' milk and that you use the best olive oil you can find!

**500g Feta cheese**
**Handful fresh mint leaves**
**1 tsp coarsely ground
  black pepper**
**1 tsp dried oregano**
**2 ripe and juicy nectarines**
**1 small punnet of
  raspberries**
**100g ripe, black olives,
  with stones**
**Extra virgin olive oil**
**Crusty bread to serve**

1. With your fingers, break up the feta into a bowl, then roughly tear the mint and mix it in, along with the oregano and the black pepper. Place the mix on a nice serving platter or bowl.

2. Slice the nectarines into wedges and arrange them on top of the feta, along with the raspberries and olives. Finish with a great big glug of olive oil and serve with crusty bread.

# 30 Wild Boar Burgers with Gorgonzola and Grilled Peaches

This will provide a real talking point to your summer BBQ! Wild boar tastes like a cross between pork and venison and in this recipe I've combined it with creamy, strong Gorgonzola cheese and gorgeous grilled peaches, for a sumptuous alternative to boring old beef burgers.

Lots of butchers and farm shops are nowadays branching out into more unusual meats, but if there's nowhere local to you, then you should find some wild boar easily enough online...

Ensure the peaches aren't over ripe, otherwise they won't hold together on the grill.

**750g minced wild boar meat**
**4 ripe peaches, flesh removed in thick slices**
**150g mountain Gorgonzola**
**4 burger buns**
**Butter**

1. Season your minced boar meat with a little salt and pepper and form into 4 nice fat burgers. Grill them well on the BBQ, but not so they dry out. At the same time, grill your peaches, basting with a little butter as you go, until they've softened and charred a little – about a minute on each side, depending how hot your BBQ is.

2. When it's all just about done, put a dollop of the Gorgonzola on each burger so it starts to melt a bit, grill off your burger buns for a few seconds, just so they get a little bit of crisp, and serve!

# 31 T-Bones with Pungent Summer Tomatoes and Crispy Roasties

This is one of my absolute favourite meals in the world. It is very simple so best ingredients are essential, especially the tomatoes – in fact, this recipe is almost the sole reason I obsessively grow tomatoes every year! If you don't grow your own, then smell before you buy – the most pungent-smelling will be the best tasting! Now, T-bone steaks are a huge indulgence with a fillet on one side of the bone and sirloin on the other, so you can of course substitute with a different cut – but nothing says STEAK like a T-bone...

**4 T-bone steaks**

**750g Maris Piper potatoes**

**2 tbsp goose fat**

**750g pungent-smelling fresh tomatoes, cut into decent sized pieces**

**6 garlic cloves, smashed with the flat of a big knife**

**3 tbsp extra virgin olive oil**

**Salt and coarsely ground black pepper**

1. Heat the goose fat in a roasting tray in the oven at 200°C.

2. Parboil the potatoes for 5-10 minutes, so they get soft around the edges but are still firm in the middle. Drain, add plenty of salt, put the lid back on and give them a good shake so they get a bit 'bashed up'. Put the roasting tray on the hob on high, so the oil stays really hot, and carefully add the potatoes. Sizzle them for 4-5 minutes, turning carefully as you go, so they start to crisp up, then put them in the oven for about 30 minutes, or until done.

3. When the potatoes are in the oven, mix the tomatoes with the garlic, a sprinkling of salt and plenty of pepper. Cover and set aside in a cool place, stirring occasionally to get the juices flowing.

4. Take your steaks out of the fridge and let them sit for 20 minutes or so, so they can come up to room temperature. Rub them in olive oil and season with salt and pepper. Sear on a very hot griddle or pan: 6 minutes on one side, 3 on the other will give you a medium-rare steak. Remove from the heat. Wrap each steak in foil and leave to rest for 5-10 minutes, by which time the potatoes should be done.

5. Serve with the potatoes on the side and the tomatoes spooned on top of the steak, along with any precious juices!

# **32** Summer Garden Party Nibbles

Forget boring old sausage rolls and cucumber sandwiches, here are some delicious nibbles that will be a real talking point for any gathering! Pick whichever ones you like the look of, or just go the whole hog and do the lot! I haven't included amounts on these as it depends on how many people you're catering for.

*Roasted Bone Marrow on Sourdough Bread with Cornichons*

**Marrow bone**
**Sourdough bread**
**Baby cornichons**

Roast the marrow bone at 180°C for 15-20 minutes or until the centre goes soft and oozy. Slice the bread into bite-sized slices or squares and lightly toast it off in the oven. Scoop the marrow out of the bones and spread it thickly on the bread, and top with a small piece of cornichon.

## Fresh Strawberries with Parmesan and Balsamic Dip

**Fresh strawberries**
**1cm cubes of Parmigiano Reggiano**
**Thick balsamic glaze**
**Coarse black pepper**

Put a strawberry and a cube of Parmesan on cocktail sticks. Give them a good crackle of black pepper and arrange on a serving plate with a dish of balsamic glaze for dipping.

## Crispy Garlic Chicken Skins

**300g chicken skins**
**Juice of ½ lemon**
**2 cloves of crushed garlic**
**Sea salt**
**Chilli flakes**

Roughly chop the garlic, mix with the chicken skins, lemon juice and a sprinkle of salt. Marinate in a covered container for 24 hours. Wipe off the chicken skins with kitchen towel and roast in a medium-hot oven for about 30 minutes, or until nice and crispy. Sprinkle in salt and chilli flakes.

## Mango, Bocconcini and Basil Skewers

**Ripe mango**
**Lime juice**
**Bocconcini mini-
 mozzarella balls**
**Basil leaves**

Cube the mango and arrange on cocktail sticks with the bocconcini and basil.

## Watermelon Lollies

**Small watermelon**
**Lolly sticks**

Cut the watermelon into thick triangles. Make a slit in the skin and insert lolly stick. Freeze for 2 hours.

*Quail Eggs, Cumin and Salt Flakes*

**Hard boiled, shelled
 quails eggs**
**Ground cumin**
**Maldon sea salt flakes**

Stick the quail eggs on cocktail sticks, and serve on a bed of sea salt and cumin.

# 33 Figgy Salmon En Croute with Watercress Salad

Fresh figs are not necessarily the first thing that springs to mind when you're thinking of what to cook with salmon, but their sweet jamminess compliments the fish perfectly in this unusual take on a classic French dish, which is served with a refreshing, peppery-mustardy watercress salad.

**500g chilled puff pastry**
**Plain flour**
**400g sustainably-fished skinless salmon fillets**
**4 large fresh figs, sliced**
**Zest of 1 lemon**
**Zest of 1 orange**
**Small sprig fresh rosemary, finely chopped – about a level tsp**
**Runny honey**
**Coarse black pepper**
**1 free-range egg, beaten**
**1 bunch watercress**
**3 tbsp olive oil**
**1 tbsp lemon juice**
**½ garlic clove, crushed**
**1 tbsp honey**
**1 tbsp wholegrain mustard**
**Pinch of salt**

1. Flour your work surface and roll out the puff pastry so that you have two equal sized sheets, big enough to cover the salmon.

2. Put one of the sheets of pastry on a piece of baking parchment and place one fillet in the middle of it. Cover with the fig slices, citrus zests, rosemary, a good drizzle of honey and a small crackle of pepper. Carefully stack your other fillet on top and press down gently.

3. Brush the pastry around the edge of the salmon with half the beaten egg. Lay your second piece of pastry on top and gently mould it around the salmon, so its nice and snug. Press around the edges with a fork to seal it well, then cut off any excess with a knife to neaten it up, making sure you leave at least a couple of centimetres. Baste with the rest of the egg. Finally, make several deep pricks into your parcel with a sharp tipped knife to allow some of the moisture to escape whilst cooking and make a nice pattern on the pastry if you like – I use a spoon to make fish-scale shapes.

4. Transfer to an oven preheated to 150°C and bake for 30 minutes or so, until nice and golden. Once done, leave to stand whilst you make your salad dressing.

5. Mix the oil, lemon juice, garlic, honey, mustard and salt in a small jug. Taste and adjust as you see fit. Pour over your watercress and serve alongside the salmon.

# 34 Chocolate Cherry Chipotle Chicken

I think if I was forced to choose, then BBQ chicken would be my number-one food in the world! This recipe is packed full of so many incredible flavours: sour cherries, smoky chipotle chillies, sweet, rich molasses and earthy dark chocolate, with just a hint of bitter coffee... a totally mouth-watering, finger-licking experience – no cutlery allowed!

Serve with a nice potato salad, or home-made coleslaw.

**40 gram dried chipotle chillies, stalks removed and roughly chopped/ shredded (remove seeds if you want less heat)**

**5 cloves of garlic, minced**

**1 tbsp dried oregano**

**1 tbsp black coffee**

**1 tbsp tomato ketchup**

**1 tbsp thick balsamic vinegar**

**2 tbsp molasses**

**100g dried cherries, roughly chopped**

**1 heaped tbsp very dark chocolate, finely grated**

**12 fresh, ripe cherries, stones and stalks removed**

**Pinch of salt**

**200ml boiling water**

**8-12 free-range, organic chicken thighs, depending on their size (and that of your guests)**

1. Put all the marinade/sauce ingredients in a food processor and pour in the boiling water. Mix well and leave to sit for half an hour, then blend until you have a smooth, fairly thick and sticky sauce.

2. Make a couple of deep cuts in each chicken thigh with a sharp knife, then place in a bowl and add the sauce, mixing really well. Cover and leave to marinate in the fridge for at least 3 hours, but preferably overnight.

3. Preheat your oven to 200°C. Place the chicken on a shallow roasting tray oven, cover in foil and cook for 45 minutes. After this time, remove the foil and cook for another 30 minutes, turning and basting in the sauce and juices regularly, until most of the liquid has gone. Allow to rest out of the oven for 10 minutes before serving, so they're cool enough to eat with fingers!

# 35 Proper Paella with Andalúz Tomato Salad

The jury's out on what makes an authentic paella, with many different camps claiming that their recipe is the most authentic. In fact paella was originally a simple peasant dish of rabbit and beans! This is the version I was taught when I worked in Madrid and it remains my favourite.

*Paella:*

300g squid, cut into rings and patted dry

4 chicken thighs, cut in half through the bone with a heavy knife or cleaver

1 medium onion, finely diced

½ green pepper, finely diced

350g paella rice

1 tbsp tomato purée

1 litre good chicken stock

1 litre good fish stock

4 cloves garlic, finely chopped

25g flat leaf parsley, chopped

Handful of frozen peas

½g saffron

1 handful fresh clams in their shells

12 fresh mussels in their shells

4 langoustine or 8 big shrimp

1 tsp salt

Good quality olive oil

Andaluz tomatoes: 8 large, ripe and strong-smelling tomatoes

2 tsp ground cumin

2 large cloves of garlic, crushed

1 romaine lettuce, leaves removed, rinsed and drained

Best extra virgin olive oil, preferably Spanish

*To serve:*

1 large crusty baguette

2 lemons, cut into wedges

1. Heat a couple of good glugs of olive oil in a 4-person paella pan, or a wide, shallow frying pan. When it's hot, add the chicken pieces and sizzle vigorously for 5 minutes, until they start to brown nicely, turning regularly using tongs.

2. Add the onion and pepper and a good pinch of salt and continue to fry for another 2-3 minutes, then add the squid for another 2-3 minutes.

3. Next, add the rice and stir for a minute, then the tomato purée, both stocks, the garlic, parsley, saffron and peas. Stir well. Bring the pan to a gentle boil and simmer, uncovered, for 15 minutes, stirring occasionally.

4. After this time, mix in the clams and mussels and lay the langoustine on top. Cook for another 10 minutes or so, turning over the langoustines half way, until the rice is cooked, topping up with boiling water as you go if necessary. (NB Top up only as much water as can be absorbed by the rice; this stops it from sticking and burning.)

5. Once it is cooked, take it off the heat and cover in a damp tea towel whilst you prepare the salad. Don't worry about rushing too much as leaving the paella to sit like this for 10 minutes or so helps it finish off nicely.

6. Slice the tomatoes into nice big chunks and mix in a bowl with the garlic, salt, cumin and olive oil. Lay out the lettuce leaves on a large plate and pour the tomatoes on top. Serve the paella in its pan on the table, along with the salad, lemon wedges and a big bowl of torn up crusty baguette.

# 36 Pulled Jerk Pork with Caribbean Mango and Papaya Salsa

I was lucky enough to work in the British Virgin Islands for a couple of years, and fell in love with the all the wonderful, vibrant cuisine the Caribbean has to offer. This recipe is a great combination of fierce, fruity scotch bonnet peppers, melt in the mouth pork and a bright, fresh, tropical salsa, all served in a soft white bun!

*Pork:*

I bunch spring onions
6 big cloves of garlic
2 scotch bonnet chillies
1 heaped tbsp fresh thyme leaves
1 tsp ground allspice
½ tsp ground cinnamon
½ tsp ground cloves
Juice of 1 orange
75ml white wine vinegar
1 tsp salt
2 tbsp dark muscovado sugar
2kg bone-in shoulder of pork
Vegetable oil

*Salsa:*

1 large ripe mango, peeled and finely diced
1 ripe papaya, peeled, seeded and finely diced
Juice of 1 lime
1 small red onion, chopped very finely
1 tbsp honey
2 mild red chillies, seeds removed and finely chopped
Handful fresh coriander, roughly chopped
8 soft white burger buns

1. Roughly chop, then blend all of the jerk marinade ingredients together in a food processor. Rub into your pork joint. Place in a suitable dish and marinate overnight in the fridge.

2. Preheat a heavy casserole in a hot oven with a couple of glugs of vegetable oil. Take the joint out of its marinating dish (reserving any juices), pop it into the casserole and cook, uncovered, for about 45 minutes, turning halfway so the outside crusts up a bit.

3. Take the casserole out the oven and turn the oven down to 140°C. Pour any marinating juices in and half a cup of water, put the lid on and cook for 6 hours.

4. When it's done, pull the meat from the bone using a combination of tongs, forks and a knife – it should come apart really easily. Put the meat back in the casserole and mix well with any cooking juices. Pop it back in the oven with the lid on and turn the oven down as low as it will go.

5. Prepare the salsa by tossing all the ingredients together in a bowl. Serve in your burger buns.

# 37 Zanderloo

Before the days of children and responsibility, we used to live on a narrowboat in the Fens. In those carefree days, I spent many an evening drinking beer and fishing with a neighbour and dear friend of mine. We caught many things, but soon discovered that the most delicious to eat was zander, and so we committed ourselves to becoming this invasive species' most fearsome predators! Zander is a scary-looking, perch-like fish with meaty, white flesh that is highly regarded throughout Europe, but only introduced to UK waters relatively recently. Luckily, due to demand from the UK's Eastern European population, zander is now more readily available to buy, but if you can't find it, then substitute with another firm, white fish.

250g Basmati rice
2 tbsp vegetable oil
1 tsp black mustard seeds
1 tsp cumin seeds
1 onion, sliced
4 tbsp best quality
  vindaloo curry paste
100ml coconut milk
2 tbsp freshly grated
  coconut
200g smooth passata
75g salted butter
4 large zander fillets,
  about 200g each
2 tbsp fresh coriander

1. Cook your basmati rice, cover and set aside so it can stay warm. Make sure it isn't over cooked, as it will be stodgy by the time you come to eat it.

2. Heat 1 tablespoon of oil in a pan and add the mustard and cumin seeds. When they start crackling, add the onion and fry until golden brown.

3. Add the curry paste, coconut milk and passata and bubble gently for about 10 minutes, stirring regularly until you have a nice, smooth sauce.

4. Heat the butter on a medium heat in a non-stick frying pan. When it starts to bubble, carefully add the fish and sauté for about 3 minutes on each side, basting well with the hot butter as you go. Just turn it once, as moving it around too much will break it up. Serve on warmed plates with the sauce poured over, a generous garnish of fresh coriander on top and fluffed up basmati rice on the side.

# 38 Autumn Duck Breast, Blackberry, Walnut and Goats' Cheese Salad

This is a wonderful meeting of autumnal flavours, with tart blackberries cutting through the richness of the duck and accompanied by new-season walnuts and fresh goats' cheese.

*Dressing:*

**175g fresh blackberries, well rinsed**

**1 tbsp good quality, thick balsamic vinegar**

**1 tbsp honey**

**2tbsp good quality extra virgin olive oil**

**1 small red onion, finely chopped**

**Pinch of salt and pepper**

*Salad:*

**4 duck breasts, skin on**

**200g chopped walnuts**

**Knob of butter**

**Large handful of blackberries, rinsed**

**300g fresh goats' cheese, such as Perroche**

**Plenty of mixed baby leaf salad**

1. To make the dressing, gently heat the blackberries in a pan until their juices are released, then squish them through a fine sieve, discarding the seeds. Allow to cool.

2. Stir in the other dressing ingredients, cover, and set aside whilst you're preparing the rest of the meal, stirring occasionally.

3. Take each duck breast and score the skin several times with a sharp knife. Season both sides with salt and pepper and then cook in a large pan, skin side down on a medium-low heat (without any added oil) for about 10-15 minutes, or until the skin is lovely and crispy. Turn them over and cook for another 2-3 minutes. Remove from the pan and set aside, uncovered.

4. Add the walnuts to the pan and stir for 4-5 minutes or until they're starting to brown, then turn off the heat.

5. Slice the duck breasts and arrange, with the goats' cheese, on the salad leaves. Top with the toasted nuts and remaining blackberries and serve with the dressing and some nice crusty bread.

# 39 Onion Soup with Armagnac and Appenzeller Cheese

Appenzeller is a hard, Gruyère-style cows' milk cheese from northeast Switzerland, with a sublime, nutty flavour. In this recipe, it is toasted on crusty bread and tops a fortifying soup made with sweet, slow-cooked onions, warming Armagnac brandy and fiery mustard.

50g butter
2 tbsp olive oil
750g mixed onions, thinly sliced
4 cloves of garlic, thinly sliced
1 tsp sugar
2 tbsp plain flour
250ml dry white wine
75ml Armagnac
2 tbsp moutarde de meaux (or a good wholegrain mustard)
1 litre beef stock
4 thick slices of crusty bread
200g grated mature Appenzeller cheese – look for *Surchoix*

1. Heat the oil and butter in a saucepan and add the onions, garlic and sugar. Cover with a lid and fry gently for 30 minutes or more, stirring frequently, until the onions are soft and sweet.

2. Sieve in the flour, stirring well as you go. Turn the heat up a bit and slowly pour in the wine, the Armagnac and then the beef stock. Bring to a very gentle bubble and leave to simmer, uncovered, for an hour or so.

3. Warm four heatproof soup bowls in the oven and turn your grill up high. Toast the bread on both sides, then ladle the soup into the bowls. Float the toast on top of the soups, smother in grated Appenzeller and put the bowls under the grill until the cheese is bubbling and brown. Serve immediately.

# 40 Penny Bun Parmigiano Risotto

Penny Bun is the English name for the mushroom *Boletus edulis*, which you most commonly hear referred to by the Italian *porcini* or French *cep*. Perhaps the most highly prized of all edible mushroom species, they grow well in the UK in all kinds of mixed woodland, but especially under pine and spruce. Every year from late September onwards, we scour the forests near us and sometimes come back with enormous hauls! If you happen to have children or grandchildren, make sure you get them involved – I find they are amazing at finding mushrooms, with their sharp eyes and endless enthusiasm, and it always turns into the most wonderful family day out! It just goes to show that wonderful food isn't necessarily about slaving away in a kitchen for hours on end. Often the best part is sourcing your ingredients!

**1 handful dried porcini mushrooms**

**Extra virgin olive oil**

**2 cloves of garlic, finely chopped**

**1 onion, chopped**

**200g fresh penny bun mushrooms, sliced 1cm thick**

**300g Vialone nano or Carnaroli rice**

**500ml chicken or vegetable stock**

**1 large glass dry white wine**

**2 tbsp flat leaf parsley, chopped**

**50g salted butter, diced**

**200g Parmigiano Reggiano (Parmesan), finely grated**

**Coarsely ground black pepper**

1. Soak your dried porcini in 250ml of very hot water for 15 minutes, then whizz up in a food processor and set aside.

2. In a large pan, gently sizzle up your onion and garlic in a generous glug of olive oil for a couple of minutes, until it's softened, then add your fresh penny buns and cook for a few more minutes.

3. Stir in the rice and mix well for a couple of minutes. Add your wine and mushroom stock and stir again. Adjust your heat if it's too slow or vigorous – you want a nice steady simmer. Once it starts bubbling, stir in a splash of the chicken stock and stir again until most of the liquid has been absorbed. Repeat this process, being careful not to let it dry out, until all the liquid has been absorbed and your rice is cooked.

4. Stir in the butter, parsley, half the Parmesan and a generous scrunch of black pepper.

5. Serve in warmed bowls, with the rest of the Parmesan on top.

# 41 Muntjac Bilberry Pie

The Muntjac deer was first introduced to the UK in the 19th Century and has steadily colonised the British countryside ever since, to the point that nowadays it's the most widely distributed of all resident deer species and is a common sight in parks, fields, gardens and roadsides. It's only relatively recently, however, with the surge in demand for interesting and unconventional meat, that it has started to become more readily available. This is a very good thing for a couple of reasons. Firstly, Muntjac are a real nuisance, causing serious damage to young trees and other plants, so keeping their numbers down really benefits the countryside. Secondly, their meat is absolutely *delicious*, often likened to a cross between venison and lamb.

The filling for this simple pie is done in the Scandinavian style, using tangy, fruity bilberries to balance out the richness of the meat. It is best served with a nice creamy mash and your favourite green vegetables, for a wonderfully hearty, warming supper.

## For the filling:

500g diced muntjac (or venison)
30g plain flour
Salt & pepper
25g butter

200g shallots
250ml venison or beef stock
200ml red wine
2 tbsp balsamic vinegar

2 bay leaves
3 heaped tablespoons bilberry jam

## For the pastry:

250g plain flour
125g salted butter, cubed and kept in the fridge

2 tbsp cold water
1 egg, beaten

Sea salt for sprinkling

## Directions for the filling

1. Sift the flour into a bowl and add a couple of pinches of salt and a good amount of pepper, mix. Add the diced muntjac and toss so it gets a good coating. Set aside.

2. Finely chop the shallots. Melt the butter in a large heavy pan or cast iron dish over a moderate heat, add the shallots and fry gently until softened.

3. Add the muntjac to the pan adding more butter if needed. Cook off for a few minutes, until the meat has seared a little.

4. Add the stock, wine, balsamic and the bay leaves. Turn the heat down and leave to bubble away happily for about an hour, stirring occasionally and scraping the bottom of the pan. When the sauce has reduced nicely, turn off the heat and stir in the bilberry jam, cover and leave until needed.

## Making the pastry

Always try to keep this brief and cold, cold, cold! If you have a food processor, all the better – just put the flour and butter in and start mixing: when it resembles breadcrumbs, slowly add the water little by little until it comes together. As soon as it has, whip the pastry out, cover with cling film and sit in the fridge to chill for at least 30 minutes before using.

If you don't have a food processor, sift the flour into a large mixing bowl and add the cold butter straight out of the fridge. Work fast, using your fingers rather than your palms to rub the butter in so that the mix resembles breadcrumbs. Slowly add the cold water, little by little, until the dough starts to come together. Quickly roll into a ball, cover with cling film and chill in the fridge for at least 30 minutes, as above.

## Making the pie

1. Bring the pastry out of the fridge to sit for 10 minutes or so to warm up a bit before rolling. Preheat the oven to 180°C. Fill your pie dish/dishes with the filling, leaving a gap at the top. Butter the rim of the dish where the pastry will sit.

2. Next, Roll out your pastry to the desired thickness (I like mine about 5mm).

3. Drape your pastry loosely over the dish and cut off, leaving a bit of overhang. Do not pull into shape or stretch it tightly to fit, as it will shrink back again! Prick the top to allow the air to escape and pinch and decorate as you like. Finally, brush with the beaten egg and sprinkle with sea salt.

4. Cook the pie in the oven for around 30-40 minutes, until the top becomes golden and crispy. Allow to sit for 10-15 minutes before serving.

# 42 Pan-Fried Partridge Breasts with Heirloom Apple Sauce

Partridge is hands down my favourite game bird and this simple recipe, full of autumnal flavours, is a lovely way to serve it. There are so many amazing fresh apples to be had at this time of year, with literally *thousands* of varieties grown in the UK. However, to find the more interesting and delicious ones, you will need to venture outside the supermarkets. We always find the best ones being sold by the side of the road and make sure we have plenty of change in the glove compartment of the car, just in case!

8 partridge breast fillets, seasoned with salt and pepper
1 large sprig of rosemary
Good glug of olive oil
Salted butter
3 medium-sized sweet apples, peeled, cored and thickly sliced
1 large red onion, peeled and finely sliced
75ml dry white wine
750g floury potatoes, such as King Edward, peeled and thickly sliced

1. Bring a pan of water to the boil and cook the potatoes until soft, but not mushy. Add a couple of generous knobs of butter and mash until smooth and creamy. Put a lid on the pan and set aside somewhere warmish.

2. Heat the olive oil in a large, flat-based pan and fry the partridge breasts with the rosemary for 3-4 minutes on each side. Remove from the pan and set aside on a warmed plate, covered with foil.

3. Melt the butter in the pan and add the apples and onion. Fry on a medium heat for about 5-6 minutes, until the apples have softened, but aren't mushy.

4. Pour in the wine and give it a good stir, making sure you give the bottom of the pan a good scraping to get up any precious juices. Bubble for a couple of minutes, until the wine has reduced a little.

5. Arrange your partridge breasts on a bed of mashed potato on warmed plates, then spoon over the apple sauce.

# 43 Saint Félicien Mini-Fondues with Kirsch Dippers

If I were to do a poll and ask all of our customers at the Cambridge Cheese company what their favourite cheese was, I'd be surprised if Saint Félicien didn't come out on top! Here, we serve it with a fiery kirsch (cherry liqueur), which cuts through the rich gloopiness of the melted cheese and warms the belly and the soul – in fact, don't be surprised if everyone starts getting a bit tipsy! I have suggested that you accompany it with hirschschinken, which is a wonderful Bavarian smoked venison with a sensational smoky flavour. A nice prosciutto di speck makes a great alternative, but you can of course use whatever charcuterie you fancy, or, indeed, a selection. This time of year is great for European grapes and Black Muscat de Hambourg are a real treat, if you can source them.

**4 individual Saint Félicien in ceramic pots**
**1 cup of kirsch**
**1 bunch Muscat de Hambourg grapes**
**200g sliced hirschschinken (smoked venison)**
**1 small loaf of sourdough bread, cut into bite-sized cubes**

1. Take any plastic off the cheese and bake in a pre-heated oven at 180°C, for about 10-15 minutes, or until it starts bubbling and forming a crust.

2. Serve the cheeses each on a small plate and put out a cup of kirsch (with more on standby!), a basket of the bread, your grapes and charcuterie. Let everyone help themselves by dipping a piece of bread in the kirsch with a fork then into the hot gooey cheese!

# 'Devilled' Pumpkin Soup

This is a hearty, spicy soup, which is served in individual pumpkin bowls. It's perfect food for when the nights are drawing and a fun addition to your Halloween supper! When we have it, we have a selection of chilli sauces to accompany it, ranging from the mild and fruity, to full-on chemical warfare... how hot can you handle?

**1kg pumpkin flesh, peeled, seeded and chopped**

**1 large carrot, coarsely chopped**

**1 medium brown onion, coarsely chopped**

**2 dried ancho chillies, coarsely chopped**

**1 sprig of thyme**

**2 tbsp olive oil**

**1 litre chicken stock**

**250ml double cream**

**2 small pumpkins or squash for bowls**

**Bread and butter**

**Chilli sauce**

1. Take your 2 small pumpkins, cut them in half and scoop out any seeds, etc. Next, hollow them out a little, so they can be used as bowls. Cut a small slice off the bottom, so that they will sit on a flat surface without tipping over. Set aside.

2. Pour the olive oil into a large, flat-bottomed pan. On a medium-high heat, add your pumpkin, carrot, onion and chilli and brown them off for about 10 minutes, stirring regularly.

3. Add the chicken stock and thyme to the pan and cover with a lid. When it starts to bubble, take the lid off and turn the heat down slightly. Allow to gently bubble away for 20-30 minutes, or until the vegetables are soft.

4. Blend the contents of your pan with a hand blender and stir in the cream. Allow to cook gently for another couple of minutes and then serve in your pumpkin-bowls, with plenty of crusty bread and butter.

# 45 Make Your Own Pizza Party

This is a really great way to spend an evening in with friends or family. Just lay out all the ingredients, put some music on, crack open some wine and let everyone create their own bespoke pizza, just how they like it! The toppings are suggestions: you can, of course, choose whatever you like.

*Pizza dough:*

**500g Italian '00' flour**
**1 7g sachet of dry yeast**
**½ tsp salt**
**350ml lukewarm water**
**1 tbsp extra virgin olive oil**

*Toppings:*

**500ml passata**
**Bocconcini (mini buffalo mozzarella balls)**
**Mature cheddar, cut into small cubes**
**Taleggio, cut into cubes**
**Gorgonzola dolce**
**Fresh goats' cheese**
**Sliced red onion/yellow pepper/garlic**
**Mixed olives, stones removed**
**Rosemary**
**Salted anchovies**
**Baby capers**
**Jalapeño peppers**
**Sliced chorizo**
**Sliced prosciutto**
**Fresh rocket**

*You will also need a basting brush for spreading the passata and plenty of greaseproof paper to cook the pizzas on.*

1. Mix the pizza dough ingredients together in a large bowl, to form a sticky dough. Turn out onto a well floured surface and knead vigorously for 5 minutes until it's silky smooth and nice and elastic. Cover the bowl in cling film and leave to rise in a warm place for an hour or more, until it has doubled in size.

2. When it's risen, knock it back by giving it another quick knead, then divide into 8 equal sized balls. With a rolling pin, roll each one as thin as it will go. Place on a suitably sized piece of greaseproof paper, dust the top with flour and then repeat, stacking each one on top of each other on a plate. Cover in cling film and set aside in the fridge until you're ready to use them.

3. Prepare all of your toppings, preheat the oven to 200°C, let everybody make their own masterpiece and cook them on the greaseproof paper. Each pizza should take about 10 minutes to cook – depending on how loaded it is!

# 46 Jamon Iberico Bellota, with Toasted Goats' Cheese, Comice Pear and Hazelnut

Jamon Iberico, or *pata negra*, is a Spanish ham which is produced from free-ranging pigs, fattened on a diet of acorns, giving the meat a unique, rich and simply exquisite flavour.

It is expensive, but worth every penny! There are several different grades available, but Bellota is best. Try and use a proper farmhouse goats' cheese made with raw milk. You want one that's firm, but not too strong, such as the French Clacbitou or Picodon; or Dorstone for a good British alternative. Comice pears are a French varietal with an exceptional flavour, but any good, large pears will do.

**150g jamon Iberico Bellota**

**1 baguette, cut into slices**

**300g goats' cheese, cut into thick slices**

**4 juicy Comice pears**

**100g shelled hazelnuts, chopped into small pieces**

**1 clove of garlic, roughly chopped**

**Hazelnut oil**

**Nice, thick balsamic vinegar**

1. Warm some hazelnut oil in a small pan and start gently toasting off your hazelnut pieces, stirring regularly. When they are starting to brown, add the garlic and stir for a couple more minutes. Remove from the heat and set aside.

2. Arrange the cheese slices on your baguette. Bake under a hot grill for about 4-5 minutes, or until the goats' cheese is browned off nicely.

3. Sprinkle the toasted nuts over the cheese, add a nice drizzle of oil and balsamic and serve immediately with your pears cut into quarters.

# 47 Ceylon Cashew Chicken with Fresh Coconut Sambal

The beautiful country of Sri Lanka (formerly Ceylon) has some of the most delicious and vibrant cuisine in the world. My best friend at school was Sri Lankan, so I was lucky to be exposed to his mum's mouth-watering home cooking from an early age. This is my take on a classic chicken curry, served with a fresh coconut sambal.

## For the sambal...

2 cloves of garlic, crushed

1 medium onion, minced or very finely chopped

2 hot green chilli, seeds removed and finely chopped

Juice of one lemon

Flesh of one coconut, finely grated

1 tsp garam masala

1 tsp coarsely ground black pepper

Pinch of salt

## For the chicken...

100g unsalted cashew nuts, shelled

1½ tbsp Garam masala

1 tsp ground cumin

1 tsp ground fenugreek

8-12 free-range chicken thighs

2cm fresh ginger root, peeled and roughly chopped

4 large garlic cloves

1 onion, roughly chopped

750ml coconut water

3 flavoursome vine tomatoes, finely chopped

30 curry leaves

Butter and vegetable oil

1. To make the sambal, blend the garlic, onion, chilli and lemon in a mini food processor. Mix well with the coconut, garam masala, salt and pepper and set aside. Stir occasionally whilst making the chicken, to help the flavours develop.

2. Clean and dry the chopper and blitz the cashews with the garam masala, cumin and fenugreek. Put them in a small frying pan and toast them VERY slowly on the lowest heat possible for about 15 minutes, stirring constantly so they don't burn. You are looking for a lovely chocolatey-brown colour. Remove from the heat and allow to cool.

3. Place a large knob of butter and a glug of vegetable oil in a big cooking pot on a medium-hot flame. Sizzle the chicken for about 10 minutes, turning occasionally.

4. Next, put the ginger, garlic and onion in the food processor and blend, slowly adding the coconut water as you go, to get a smooth consistency. Add to the pan with the chicken. Bring to the boil, then add the tomato, the toasted spice mix and the curry leaves. Turn it down to a gentle bubble and cook, uncovered, for about 40 minutes, or until done.

# 48 Levantine Rice Kubba

Kubba or Kibbeh are popular all over the Middle East. Shells of rice or bulgar wheat are stuffed with delicious fillings and then deep fried until golden. I've used a traditional lamb mince filling, in a rice shell in the Iraqi style, but you can fill them with whatever you like – try feta, mint and black olives for a vegetarian alternative.

## Shell:

**300g short grain rice**
**1 tsp turmeric**
**1 large free-range egg, beaten**

## Filling:

**250g minced lamb**
**1 tsp cumin seeds**
**½ tsp turmeric**
**½ tsp ground cinnamon**
**½ tsp ground allspice**
**100g almonds, chopped**
**1 tbsp sultanas, chopped**
**1 small onion, finely chopped**
**1 clove garlic, finely chopped**
**Salt and pepper**
**1 heaped tbsp chopped parsley**
**1 heaped tbsp chopped mint**
**Plenty of vegetable oil for deep frying**

## Yoghurt dip:

**3 heaped tbsp natural yoghurt**
**1 small garlic clove**
**1 tsp chopped parsley**
**Good squeeze of lemon juice**

1. To make the shells, first soak the rice for 30 minutes and rinse. Then cook the rice in plenty of water with the turmeric for a bit longer than you might normally, until it's really soft. Drain very well, squeezing out any excess water – if you have a fine cloth to do this with, all the better: you want to really wring it dry. Allow to cool. Give the rice a bit of a mashing, but not so it's a purée – you want to keep some of its texture. You could also pulse it in a food processor until you get the desired consistency. Next, beat in the egg and using damp hands knead into a smooth dough. Divide it into 8 roughly equal balls and chill in the fridge for 30 minutes.

2. Fry the onion in a little oil until it's softened, then add the mince. Fry until browned: about 5-10 minutes. Add the rest of the ingredients, except the fresh herbs, and cook for another 5 minutes. When it's all cooked, stir in the herbs and allow to cool.

3. Make the yoghurt dip by combining all the ingredients and mixing together. Transfer to a serving bowl and set aside in the fridge.

4. Place a bowl of water on your work surface for your hands; you'll want to keep them moist as you handle the dough. Take one of the rice balls and flatten it into a disc on your palm. Put a spoonful of the stuffing in the middle and close the shell around it, smoothing off the edges and sealing it well.

5. Repeat the process with all the balls. When they're all prepped and ready, deep fry in very hot oil until they're a lovely golden colour. Remove with a slotted spoon and place onto paper to drain any excess oil. Serve hot with the yoghurt dip.

# 49 Baked Halibut with Citrus Salad and Crushed New Potatoes

This is a wonderfully vibrant dish, full of sparkling colours and intense flavours. The mix of juices from the fish, the citrus fruits, fresh mint, onion and olive oil all soak into the crushed new potatoes for a totally mouth-watering experience! I love halibut, but it can have a tendency to dry out, so baking it in foil really helps to trap in the moisture and the flavour.

**6 ripe oranges**

**2 lemons**

**2 limes**

**1 small red onion, thinly sliced**

**25g fresh mint, roughly chopped**

**25g flat leaf parsley, roughly chopped**

**3 tbsp strongly flavoured, extra virgin olive oil**

**Coarsely ground pepper**

**750g new potatoes**

**Sea salt crystals**

**4 150-200g halibut steaks or fillets**

**1 extra lemon**

1. Peel your fruit. Then, with a sharp knife, over a bowl to catch any juice, cut out the flesh from the skin of each segment of the oranges, lemons and limes. Mix in the onion, herbs, olive oil and pepper. Cover and set aside in the fridge whilst you're getting everything else ready.

2. Heat your oven to 180°C. Put the potatoes on a roasting tray with a good glug of olive oil and a liberal sprinkling of coarse sea salt.

3. Wrap each individual piece of halibut in foil, with a slice of lemon, and put them in the oven on a shelf below the potatoes. After 20 minutes, take out your fish and leave in their foil to keep warm. Turn the oven up high and carry on cooking the potatoes until the skins have gone nice and brown and a bit crispy.

4. Put the cooked potatoes in a bowl and crush (not so much that they're mashed!). Arrange on warmed plates, along with the fish. Give the citrus salad a good stir and spoon on top.

# 50 Basque Egg Piperade

After a long and troublesome journey to the Pyrenees a few years ago, we arrived feeling hungry and exhausted. However, the simple supper of slow-cooked peppers and eggs with big chunks of crusty sourdough bread that our wonderful hostess had prepared for us soon revived our spirits and will always stick in my memory as one of the best and gratefully received meals I have ever eaten!

The dish is flavoured with Espelette peppers, a Basque speciality with a smoky-sweet flavour and a gentle heat.

**2 red, 1 yellow and 1 green pepper, stalks, seeds and pith removed and thinly sliced**

**1 large onion, peeled and thinly sliced**

**3 garlic cloves, crushed**

**1 tin best quality chopped tomatoes**

**250ml water**

**1 tbsp dried Piment d'Espelette powder (or Spanish pimenton)**

**2 bay leaves**

**Extra virgin olive oil**

**4 free-range eggs**

**One small tin of salted anchovies, preferably Cantabrian (or best available)**

**1 loaf of sourdough bread, cut into large chunks**

1. Preheat your oven to 150°C.

2. Heat some olive oil in a pan and add the peppers, onion and garlic. Sweat them off gently with a lid on for 10 minutes, then add the tomatoes, water, dried pepper and bay leaves and cook very gently for about 45 minutes to an hour, or until most of the liquid has evaporated, stirring frequently so it doesn't stick or burn. When it's ready, serve it into preheated (hot) bowls.

3. Pop your bread in the oven on a tray so it can crisp up a bit. (Keep a bit of an eye on it so it doesn't burn.)

4. Get some more oil nice and hot in non-stick pan and fry your eggs. You want a slightly crispy white and, most importantly, a runny yoke. I find the best way is to splash hot oil from the pan over the top of them with a spoon while they're frying.

5. Transfer the eggs to the tops of the soups and drape with anchovies. Serve with lovely crusty bread and extra olive oil, if desired!

# **51** Guyanese Garlic Pork

My mouth is watering just thinking about this recipe... it is a traditional Guyanese dish, served at special occasions and was first introduced to me by a dear friend of mine whose mum is Guyanese. This is my version – it's pretty simple, but does take a few days of marinating, so you'll need to get on it in advance... I promise it's worth it!

**12 large garlic cloves, crushed roughly in their skins with a rolling pin**

**6 branches of fresh thyme**

**5 cloves**

**1 Habañero or Scotch bonnet pepper, chopped, seeds and all!**

**1 kg pork belly, cut into 1 inch cubes**

**2 tsp table salt**

**1.5 litre cider vinegar**

**Plenty of vegetable oil for cooking**

**Soft white bread rolls and butter**

*You will also need a 2 litre Kilner jar.*

1. Layer the garlic, thyme, cloves, habañero, pork and salt in your Kilner jar and pour over the vinegar. Give it a gentle shake to mix it all up and get the flavours working. Top up with extra vinegar if necessary, close the jar and marinate in the fridge for 3-4 days, turning it and giving it a gentle shake from time to time, to keep the flavours mingling!

2. Once the pork has been pickled, drain the liquid off, but keep the garlic, thyme, etc., with it. Dry it all out on paper towels, removing as much extra moisture as possible.

3. Heat about 2 cm of oil in a large, flat-bottomed pan. It needs to be hot, so test it with one small piece of pork first – it should sizzle vigorously as soon as it touches the oil. Fry the rest of the pork, along with the marinade ingredients, in batches (don't over-crowd the pan), until it is nice and brown (about 15 minutes). Lay your cooked pork out on paper towels as you go to soak up any excess oil before serving.

4. Serve in buttered bread rolls.

# 52 Roast Goose with Tamarillo Jelly, White Truffle Butter, Crispy Roasties & Pan-Fried Sprouts with Bacon

Pull out all the stops this Christmas and wow your guests with this opulent dinner. Tangy, exotic tamarillo jelly cuts through the richness of the goose and the ambrosial white truffle! Potatoes are roasted to crispy perfection in goose fat and served with pan-fried sprouts and bacon.

*For the tamarillo jelly (best made a few days in advance...)*

**1kg fresh tamarillos, cut into quarters**
**Juice of 1 lemon**
**750ml water**
**500g granulated sugar**

1. Place the tamarillos, lemon juice and water in a large saucepan. Bring to a gentle boil and simmer, uncovered, for an hour.

2. Line a large sieve with a muslin cloth. Position it on top of a bowl and pour in the contents of the saucepan. Select a plate that's a bit smaller in diameter than the sieve and place it on top. This will help squeeze the juice out very gently and slowly. Leave to strain overnight.

3. Measure the amount of liquid left and pour it into a clean pan. Add an equal amount of sugar (for example 500ml of liquid will need 500g of sugar) and bring to a rolling boil. Bubble vigorously for about 20 minutes, until setting point is reached. The best way to check this is to put a plate in the freezer and when it's very cold, spoon a very small amount of your jelly onto it. Run your finger through it: if it separates and stays separate, rather than running back together, then it's thick enough. Pour into sterilised jars.

*For the goose and vegetables...*

**4-5kg goose, prepared**

**2 lemons, quartered**

**2 onions, quartered**

**1kg floury potatoes, peeled and cut into roast potato-sized pieces**

**A couple of sprigs of rosemary**

**4 thick slices of smoked bacon, cut into thin, short strips**

**2 tbsp unsalted butter**

**500g Brussels sprouts, cut in half**

**1 jar white truffle butter**

1. Remove any excess fat from the cavity of the goose, season and stuff with the onions and lemons. Use a skewer to prick the bird all over.

2. Preheat the oven to 180°C. Place the goose in a roasting tray and cover well with foil. Put it in the oven and cook for 2 hours 30 mins, basting every 30 minutes and draining off excess fat into a large, heatproof bowl as you go.

3. After this time, remove the foil and cook for a further 30 minutes, so the goose browns up nicely. Take the goose out of the oven and loosely cover in foil. It will stay perfectly warm while you prepare the vegetables.

4. Parboil the potatoes, then drain, add plenty of salt, put the lid back on and give them a good shake so they get a bit 'bashed up'. Turn the oven up high. Put the roasting tray, with a couple of good glugs of your reserved goose fat, on the hob. Turn it up high, so the oil gets really hot and carefully add the potatoes, along with your rosemary. Sizzle for 4-5 minutes, turning carefully as you go, so the potatoes start to crisp up. Then put them in the oven for about 30 minutes, or until done.

5. When the potatoes are getting close to being ready, sizzle up the bacon in a large frying pan until it's crispy. Remove from the pan and drain on some kitchen towel. Add the butter to the pan and cook the sprouts on a medium-high heat for about 10 minutes, or until golden brown. Remove from the heat and stir in the bacon.

6. Bring the goose to the table and carve. Let people help themselves to vegetables and lashings of tamarillo jelly and truffle butter.

Merry Christmas!!

# Image credits

**Martin Denny:** *Freshly picked St George's mushrooms (page 13).*

**Camilla Marshall-Lovsey:** *Turmeric butter chicken – finished dish (page 19); Russian morel chicken – finished dish (page 35); Home made bangers and brown sauce (page 43); Pulled jerk pork with Caribbean mango and papaya salsa (page 109); Autumn duck breast, blackberry, walnut and goats' cheese salad (page 115).*

**Shannon Shafer:** *Mulato chile burritos (page 25); Chocolate cherry chipotle chicken (page 103).*

**Jade Thomas:** *Fabada Asturiana (page 41); Cream tea with rose petal jam (page 81); Pan-fried partridge breasts with heirloom apples (page 129); Levantine rice kubba (page 143).*

**Pata Negra Foods:** *Pigs (page 138); Iberico ham (page 139).*

*From Shutterstock:*

   **Godrick**: *Parmesan wheels (page 118).*

   **Agnes Kantaruk**: *Baked goose (page 154).*

   **Magnago**: *Traditional French dish tartiflette (page 39).*

   **Kate Nag**: *Fresh fruit tamarillo (page 156).*

   **Lisovskaya Natalia**: *Onion soup (page 117).*

   **Pictoplay**: *Fine looking zander (page 112).*

   **Alphonsine Sabine**: *Indian meatballs with curry sauce – finished dish (page 47); Risotto with wild mushrooms – finished dish (page 121).*

   **stockcreations**: *Haggis and vegetables (page 23).*

   **Toniflap**: *Typical Spanish seafood paella (page 106).*

   **zi3000**: *Creamy pumpkin soup – finished dish (page 133).*

*All other images by the author.*